PIGS
& WILD BOARS

A PORTRAIT OF THE ANIMAL WORLD

BEN SONDER

TODTRI

This book was designed and produced by TODTRI Book Publishers
P.O. Box 572, New York, NY 10116-0572 FAX: (212) 695-6984

Printed and bound in Korea

ISBN 1-57717-081-4

Author: Ben Sonder

Publisher: Robert M. Tod
Editor: Edward Douglas
Assistant Editor: Elaine Luthy
Book Designer: Mark Weinberg
Typesetting: Command-O Design

PHOTO CREDITS
Photo Source/Page Number

Michael H. Black 19 (top), 21

Bruce Coleman, Inc. 28
Mark Boulton 68–69
Rick Buettner 19 (center)
Kenneth W. Fink 56–57
M.P.I. Fogden 59 (bottom)
Lee Foster 29 (bottom)
Michael P. Gadomski 3, 6 (top), 20 (top)
Malcolm Harris 7
M. P. Kahl 61
David Madison 59 (top)
Lynn M. Stone 34, 39
Frank Oberle 14 (bottom)
Hans Reinhard 15
Steve Solum 13 (top & Bottom)
Kim Taylor 60 (bottom)
Nicholas de Vore III 42 (bottom), 43

M. Timothy O'Keefe 16

Photo Researchers, Inc.
Alan D. Carey 35
Tim Davis 29 (top)
Nigel Dennis 45
Fletcher & Baylis 52–53
Holt Studios International/Nigel Cattlin 22, 26 (top), 27, 49
William J. Jahoda 66 (bottom)
M. P. Kahl 58
Tom McHugh 23, 33, 47 (top), 55, 66 (top), 67, 70
G. Carleton Ray 44
St. Meyers/Okapia 46–47, 48, 50, 51
Bonnie Rauch 24–25, 31 (top)
Mitch Reardon 64, 65 (bottom)
Leonard Lee Rue III 63

Picture Perfect 11, 36–37, 71
C. K. Amman 65 (top)
Nick Gurgul 5
Eric Riddick 6 (bottom),

Tom Stack & Associates
Warren Garst 60 (top)
Gary Milburn 46 (left)
John Shaw 62
Inga Spence 26 (bottom), 30, 31 (bottom), 38 (top)
Roy Toft 54

Lynn M. Stone 4, 8–9, 10, 12, 14 (top), 17, 18, 19 (bottom),
20 (bottom), 32 (top & bottom), 37 (right), 40–41, 42 (top)

INTRODUCTION

By turning over sun-dried earth to reveal the mud underneath, these pigs are receiving a double benefit. The moist earth is likely to contain more succulent nutrients than the parched top-soil. And because wet earth is cooler, it helps to lower the pigs' body temperature.

Throughout history people have associated various animals with certain human perceptions. The lion was seen as a noble beast; the tiger, a savage killer; and the dog, a loyal and faithful friend. In its turn, the pig has been, mistakenly but understandably, considered filthy, greedy, and dim. However, the pig is one of the most intelligent mammals outside of the primates and a rival of the dog in its ability to become attached to people.

It takes a zoologist to understand fully how closely the body systems of the human and the pig resemble each other, and nowadays only those who raise pigs in numbers small enough for intimate interaction understand the rather remarkable emotional and intellectual complexities of this animal. But on small farms today, as in the past, pigs are often treated as beloved family members before they are slaughtered, or at least they become the family's principal pet.

A pig loves to be scratched and petted, and once it has given an individual a thorough olfactory examination, might even be disposed to a nose-butting that resembles a kiss. Over the course of their interactions with humans, pigs develop complex relationships based on love or fear, feeding routines, and familiarity with scents.

Pigs have a variety of "language" skills, being able to express their needs and emotions in predictable and understandable vocal ways. A domestic pig will bark to send a warning, squeal when it is frightened, shriek when it is in pain, and grunt either to show aggression or express feelings of contentment. So resourceful is the pig, that it has been known to open the latches of barn doors with its snout to reach food or a sweetheart. And of course, the superior sense of smell of pigs makes them peerless truffle-finders in the Perigord region of France. They can locate these delicacies beneath the ground as far as 20 feet (6 meters) away.

Because of their olfactory ability, pigs were sometimes substituted for hunting dogs in England at the beginning of the nineteenth century, and the tradition of training pigs to sniff out objects humans can't find continues. Pigs have also been used to locate contraband drugs and to find land mines during wartime.

Most female pigs have excellent mothering instincts that are bound to inspire tender feelings in humans. Before giving birth, both a domestic and a wild female pig will carefully build a comfortable nest from hay, leaves,

moss, or weeds. Once her litter is born, she will remain in this nest to feed it—eating little herself, if necessary—for as long as two weeks. Afterwards, she will introduce her offspring to the outside world, where they will continue to be nurtured by all the females in the group.

As pets and performers, some species of pigs are highly trainable. However, despite the many talents of pigs, people persist in promoting stereotypes that associate pigs with filth, greed, and ugliness. All of us are aware of these associations and may find ourselves unthinkingly advancing them in conversation. However, insinuating that pigs are the epitome of uncleanness simply reveals a misconception. In actuality, pigs rank as one of the cleaner animals on a farm. If allowed, they tend to defecate in the same spot and prefer it

Like dogs and cats, pigs are noted for their ability to communicate their feelings. The pleasure these two piglets take from each other's company is clear, as they come together to exchange greetings.

Pigs are sociable animals, liable to greet passersby at the gate to the barn door; or, they may hoist themselves up for a little sightseeing, to break up the day's routine. Sometimes special security precautions are needed to keep them where they belong.

A European domestic hog bides its time at a zoo in Tacoma, Washington. Some hogs have perpetually runny eyes, caused by extremely active tear ducts. If allowed to, hogs like this can reach weights of well over a thousand pounds (450 kilograms).

Pigs confined to a sty may spend hours gazing at the outside world. Sometimes they're cunning and strong enough to break out of their confinement and wander off to root for plants.

Pigs of substantial girth, such as this sow nibbling a snack in a Swedish farmyard, have become extremely popular in recent years. Their sleek coats, large size, and bulky shape have made them well-loved pets.

to be located at a distance from their sleeping and living areas. It is true that pigs will wallow in mud, but only if they are deprived of clean water to bathe in or damp earth to roll in. Because they have no sweat glands, their only way of cooling their body is by evaporation. They have a need for frequent wettings, especially in hot weather. So essential is this to their survival that when there is no other way of cooling off, they have no choice but to roll in their own excrement.

Another thing many people don't realize is that pigs are not greedy. Because of their girth and muscle mass, they require large amounts of water, protein, and carbohydrates to stay healthy. They are primarily attracted to grains, grasses, peas, or roots, but they will also eat scraps of meat, grains, fruit, and vegetables that come from the table. This doesn't mean, however, that their developed olfactory glands and taste buds have not endowed them with strong preferences.

As for the beauty or ugliness of pigs, it can only be said that aesthetics is in the eye of the beholder. An understanding of the amazing functionality of pigs' snouts—for digging and rooting—as well as an appreciation of their keen sense of smell, might make them more appealing to those who say they dislike the pig's nose. Domestic pigs do have a tendency toward plumpness, but that doesn't mean such a silhouette can't be graceful. Wild boars are leaner, however, with rather thin legs. Perhaps the most endearing thing about some pigs is their eyes. Sight is not their keenest sense, and their eyes are rather small in proportion to the rest of their body, but there seems to be a docile quality about the eyes that lends a certain gentleness and sweetness to pigs' faces.

Following page: While suggesting to the viewer the traditional presentation of a pig as a main course at a great banquet, this hog poses happily for the camera.

DOMESTIC PIGS

Pigs belong to the modern family of Suidae in the order Artiodactyla, which comprises all the hoofed animals with an even number of toes including deer, sheep, cattle, and camels. The Suidae are divided into five genera, some of which are *Barbirussa*, the genus of the babirusa, an Indonesian, four-tusked pig; *Phacochoerus*, the genus of warthogs; and *Sus*, the genus of so-called true pigs, which, among others, contains the domestic pig and its ancestor the wild boar. The Suidae are related to the Tayassuidae, the family of peccaries, and together the two families form the infraorder Suina, or swine.

True pigs have existed for at least 45 million years. Today, there are various species in every continent except Antarctica. These omnivores survive on farms or in the wild, where they live on a diet of roots, fungi, fruit, snails, reptiles, eggs, carrion, and other types of available food, which they root out of the ground, if necessary, with their snouts. Some, such as the pygmy hog of India, are endangered, and others, such as the Javan warty pig and the Vietnam warty hog, are nearly extinct. Still others, such as the endangered Visayan warty pig of the Philippines, lead secret lives, barely documented by zoologists.

Anatomy
Members of the family Suidae have simple stomachs and as a rule do not ruminate, or chew the cud. Their canines keep growing and sometimes form tusks. They have a mobile snout, with a disk of cartilage that can be used for digging. Most pigs have poor eyesight. Their body is covered with bristles. Females are usually frequent reproducers, with many teats and large litters.

Since they enjoy grasses, pigs can be left to feed in a pasture during the warm months of the year. However, in the following year, they must be sent to another area, to allow the previous year's pasture to regrow.

Domestic pigs are familiar to most of us, but it is likely that most people have never given specific thought to the all of the features that distinguish these animals from others. The domestic pig has four toes on each foot, with very thick nails. Two of the toes on each foot are reduced in length and do not touch the ground. The pig's eyes are small and close together and its large, floppy ears give it an acute sense of hearing. Domestic pigs have sharp, pointed teeth, good for crunching seeds or roots and for tearing grasses and hay. They are major nibblers, and some have, on rare occasions, given serious bites to people. Their tails have a corkscrew curl, although many raisers remove the tips of these by docking to prevent them from being bitten off by other pigs.

One characteristic that makes domestic pigs valuable to farmers is that they gain weight quickly. By the time a piglet is weaned, it has already increased its weight tenfold. In six months it is market ready, at a weight of about 220 pounds (100 kilograms). Those pigs that are allowed to live longer easily reach weights over 1,000 pounds (450 kilograms).

The terminology concerning domestic pigs can be confusing. In general, *swine* can be used to refer to any member of the species. In

With small, rather weak eyes, pigs often appear to be squinting at the world. This behavior can give their faces an expressiveness intriguing to humans. A pig's gaze, on occasion, may appear wistful or long suffering, and at other times, all-knowing and sadly ironic.

America, the word *hog* means a large domestic pig, usually 120 pounds (55 kilograms) and over. *Boar* sometimes refers to a wild pig from the same species as the domestic pig. However, when breeders use the term, they are referring to a sexually mature male domestic pig. *Barrows* are castrated males, intended for the pork market. Older female domestic pigs that have already given birth to a litter are called *sows*. *Weaners* or *shoats* are weaned farm pigs that weigh 25 to 40 pounds (12 to 18 kilograms).

The Domestication of Pigs

European wild boars, the ancestors of the domestic pig, once roamed the forests of Europe in large numbers, but hunters who fancied their meat nearly depleted their population. However, in recent years, conservation efforts have partially replaced their population in the wild and some are used as breeding animals. Humans are responsible for the taming and breeding of wild boars, which led to the development of the domestic pig. Semi-domestication of pigs may already have

Completely oblivious to its surroundings, a pig dozes in the late afternoon sun. During the hottest days of the summer, these animals must be provided with ample areas of shade, since they are unable to regulate their body heat naturally.

An Old World domestic hog wallows in a luxurious bath of mud, the relief on its face evident. If given the choice, it might prefer clearer water. However, one advantage of mud over water is that mud sticks to the body and evaporates more gradually.

A European domestic swine seeks relief from the heat by rolling in mud. Old World domestic swine often resemble the wild boar more than the American varieties do. Their snouts tend to be longer and their coats hairier.

Since pigs can be destructive to crops as they root up the earth in search of food, rings are often attached to their snouts to discourage this activity.

begun as early as 7000 B.C. in Neolithic culture. Early peoples with herds of pigs were also likely to have used pigs as living plows, letting them clear forest land for farming by the incessant rooting they love to do with their snouts. Before that period, humans hunted wild pigs, as evidenced by the pictures of boars painted on the walls of Cro-Magnon caves.

Columbus brought eight pigs to Haiti in 1493, and descendants of these were taken from the West Indies to the mainland by other explorers. In both environments their numbers increased rapidly. Then, in the seventeenth century, settlers brought pigs to the American colonies, where they were often allowed to roam wild in the woods. Periodically, the settlers would capture and slaughter them, and they became an important source of meat, lard, leather, and bristles. Most of the feral pigs that exist on the American continent today are partial descendants of domestic breeds.

In the eighteenth century, Robert Bakewell of Leicestershire crossed a large European pig with the smaller Chinese variety. The result was a very fat pig that was rich in lard. Up to the 1920s, lard was considered a major resource supplied by the pig. Farm pigs in Europe and the United States tended to be like Bakewell's hybrid—fat and jowly with short legs. After lard lost its preeminence as a cooking ingredient, pigs were bred to be more muscular and leaner than in the past. Now their shoulders and hams, which contain plenty of meat, are extremely important to producers.

Communication between pigs takes many forms, not all of which are completely understood by humans. A kiss between generations may be a sign of affection, but could also be an adult's way of using its sense of smell to determine the recent whereabouts or current health of a piglet.

Domestic pigs are very resourceful in conserving body heat and staying comfortable. This hog has found a secluded corner of the barn where the hay is abundant enough to provide warmth and cushioning. It's the perfect place for an afternoon nap.

Commercial Value

The United States has a large number of domestic pigs, second only to China, which has one-third of the total world population. For the agricultural industry, pigs have many advantages. They grow quickly and can produce a large litter twice a year. Because they are omnivores, there is a wide range of food that can be used to feed them. Aside from their meat, they offer an array of useful products that includes pigskin leather, bristles for brushes, and wood glue. In addition, pigs supply the medical industry with heart valves that can be implanted in humans, and skin that is used to dress serious burns without using

The wild boar is the immediate ancestor of the feral hog of North America (shown here). Today, this old story takes a new turn, as wild boars are imported to Canada to be raised and marketed as a prestige meat for the up-scale, specialty food market.

adhesive. Because the biochemical processes of the pig resemble those of humans, they can produce pituitary gland extract, a thyroid hormone, insulin, and heparin for human use.

These days the $5 billion industry of pig farming—sending 75 million pigs to market yearly—has reached high-tech, mass-production proportions. It's a three-pronged enterprise that involves the production of purebreds for breeding; the breeding of feeder pigs, which tend not to be purebred; and the raising of pigs for slaughter. Large-scale farming may approach these three activities using different strategies. Some farmers are solely responsible for all three. Others belong to cooperatives where the pigs are bred and weaned, then fed and finished back at home. Large-scale pig raising today also requires a number of specialists, including veterinarians and nutritionists. The latter are absolutely essential, because the majority of production costs are for feed. It takes about 400 pounds (180 kilograms) of feed to produce a pig weighing 100 pounds

Though pigs are enjoyed as companions and pets, they are even more prized for their economic value. Relatively inexpensive to raise, they provide an abundance of products, from meat and lard to pigskin and bristles.

(45 kilograms). Pigs raised in numbers of a thousand or more under crowded conditions also have to be protected by vaccination, antibiotics, and on-the-spot treatment for various diseases. What is more, pigs need proper ventilation to keep cool in warm weather and warm in cold weather, and to keep from being poisoned by the gases that come from their waste products.

Large-scale pig production usually mandates total confinement for pigs. Slotted floors collect manure, which is removed daily. Heating and cooling systems are substituted for hay and mud holes. However, even some large-scale operations do use the pasture method, mainly because grazing supplies pigs with about 15 percent of their food requirements.

When pigs are given the opportunity to roam about at will, they are rewarded with a wide variety of foods. Here, three pigs have come across some newly fallen apples and are enjoying the rare treat.

Small Farms

On small-scale pig farms, which still exist today for both fun and profit, pig raising takes on a more humane or, at least, a more traditional face. In many cases, pigs are allowed to enjoy pasture, and piglets may interact with humans the ways puppies would. Shelters and fences for pigs, as well as the areas in which they are allowed to roam, vary, depending on the finances and commitment of the small farmer. One fact these small farmers keep in mind is that the more confined a pig is, the more money and upkeep it will entail, and the more unhappy the pig will be. For one thing, social interactions between pigs are not always smooth. Competition and fighting among pigs can lead to injuries.

The English countryside has long been known for its rustic beauty and simplicity, with its picturesque, well-kept fields dotted with grazing livestock. In this picture, a herd of rooting pigs is the star attraction.

At a farm-park in North Avon in England, two saddleback hogs, of substantial weight and size, raise themselves up to observe the day's activities. The natural curiosity of pigs indicates their considerable degree of intelligence.

On farms with just several pigs, modified confinement is usually the answer. There is a fenced-in, outside pasture, or pen area, and a housing area, with heat and cooling systems if necessary. Others, for ethical, traditional, or practical reasons, offer their pigs large pastures of alfalfa or clover with only a shed for protection from the elements. Up to thirty-five hogs can be satisfied with an acre of pasture. Here the pigs can romp, spending the day at play and incessant rooting, cooling their backs in areas where the grass or earth is damp, rolling in streams, or digging their own mud holes. During the spring, summer, and fall they require little else but shade and some straw or hay for bedding.

However, hogs are rarely grazed on the same pasture year after year. The pasture needs a chance to regrow after a season of rooting. To slow pasture damage, some raisers ring the noses of mature pigs. The procedure consists of fastening one or two rings above each nostril, or through the cartilage between the nostrils. This hampers the ability of the animal's snout to turn up a large amount of soil.

Pigs are intelligent, curious animals with strong needs, and they are prone to wander. Weaners have been known to squeeze through small holes in fences, and large pigs have simply crashed through them. It's easy to push a fence down if its boards are nailed to the outside. All sizes of pigs may nibble patiently at a

Since they easily become attached to humans, pigs on small-scale farms often win the affection of their keepers. This is especially true of farm children, who enjoy feeding and caring for these gentle creatures.

Even though most food source animals are now grown in industrial fashion on a massive scale, there are still a number of small farms, both in Europe and North America, that raise farm animals, including pigs, by time honored, traditional methods. In less developed areas, that depend on subsistence agriculture, pigs are a valuable economic resource.

When for both ethical and practical reasons, pigs are given the run of a large pasture, they are free to behave in all the ways that are natural to them. In addition to rooting up the ground for food, they greet each other, romp and play, bathe in water, and dig their own mud holes.

fence until a space large enough for an escape has been created. Others even jump or climb over. To prevent such escapes, farmers sometimes use electrical fencing. In a few cases, however, an owner doesn't mind where a pig roams. It may acquire the status of a mascot in the area, making regular visits to neighbors in town who provide treats and attention.

Despite the fact that pigs receive some of their nutrition through grazing, they still need to be fed. Many pig raisers now use mechanized self-feeders, but there are some small-scale pig farmers who enjoy feeding their pigs by hand. These people usually pour food into the troughs two to four times a day, taking care to provide a balanced diet. A feed base of corn and other grains, supplemented with peas, root crops, squash, and fruit, as well as protein from milk and eggs, keep a pig well nourished.

On a farm in the county of Devon in southwestern England, a farmer has set up what is described as a "humane, free-range system" for his animals. Seen here are Devonshire dumpling pigs, that are not only content, but reportedly quite friendly.

A large white Landrace and some Duroc piglets graze. Metal hutches in the pasture provide protection from the heat of the sun. The grasses and roots these hogs eat provide important nourishment. However, in order to thrive, they will need heavy supplements of grain-based feed.

Pig Breeds

Few pedigreed pigs end up at market. The purebreds are raised for crossbreeding purposes. They provide proven genes that can be used in creating pigs for specific niches of the market. Some purebreds, however, are shown at fairs and livestock shows. The genetic background of a pig matters to its raiser. Each breed has distinct qualities that affect its behavior, the kind of care it requires, and the kind of profit it will yield.

Berkshire

The Berkshire is one of the oldest breeds of domestic pigs. It originated in Berkshire, England, in 1789, and came to the United States thirty-four years later. These pigs are black with white on their face and feet. They are medium-sized with smooth bristles and a meaty body. Their faces resemble that of a pug dog, and their ears are very erect. Berkshires mature early, although they do not breed as enthusiastically as some other types of pigs.

They are sturdy, rugged animals that make good crossbreeders.

Chester White

Chester Whites are "full-blooded Americans." Although they are genetically related to several English breeds of pigs, they first originated in Chester County, Pennsylvania, near the beginning of the nineteenth century. They are white-bristled, with pink skin and forward-flopping ears. Chester Whites make good grazers and especially good mothers. Raisers value them for their lean meat.

Duroc

This breed got its name in 1823 when a New York State farmer named Isaac Frink bought two large pigs from a man with a stallion named Duroc. The pigs were a cross between Jersey reds and some New York breeds. Durocs have floppy ears. They're aggressive and hardy, and the females are good breeders. These intelligent pigs grow more quickly than most breeds.

Boar-Mangalizas, or Golden Boars, are characterized by dense yellowish fur that resembles the fleece of a sheep. This is a very old breed, originating in the ancient Roman province of Pannonia, which covered parts of present-day Austria, Hungary, and Slovenia.

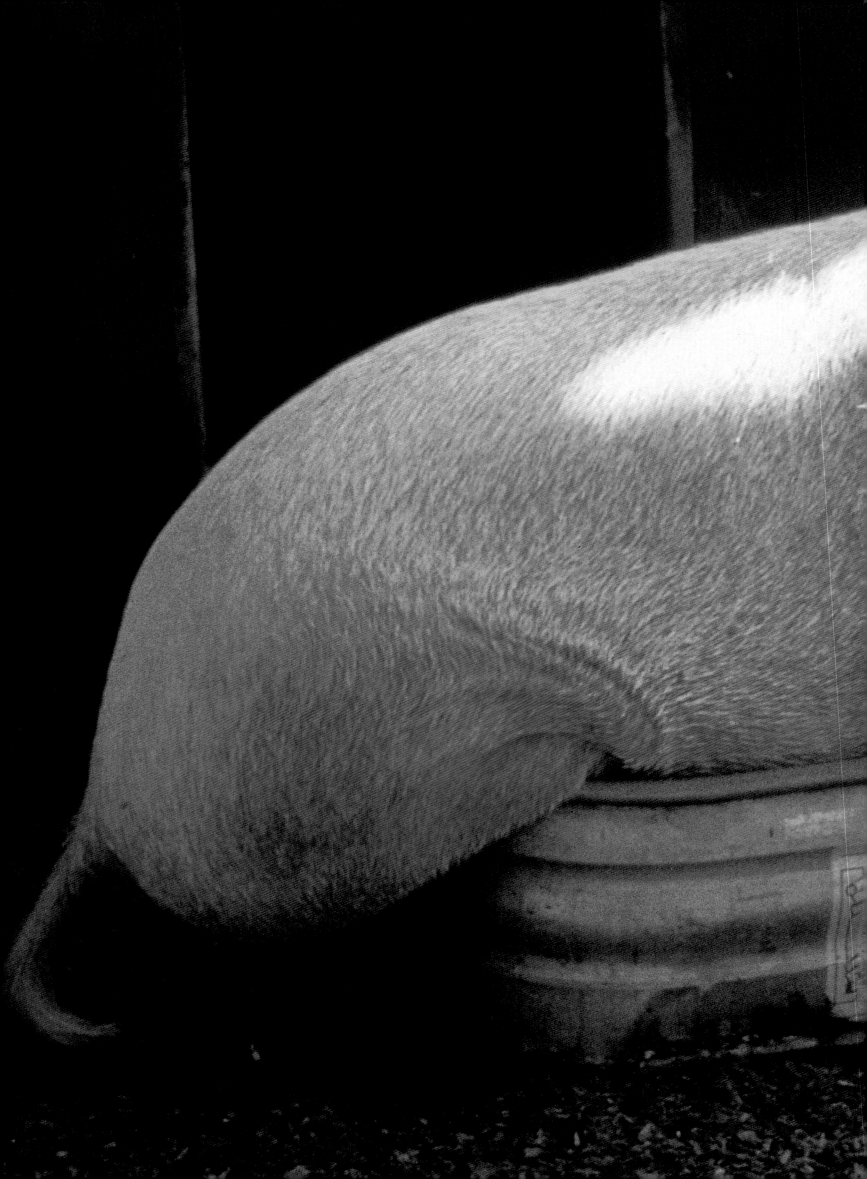

Because they do not perspire, hogs bathe, then allow the water to evaporate and cool their bodies. This large white Landrace and its piglets are enjoying water from a hose set up in an outdoor breeding unit. Fresh water for bathing and drinking is of prime importance during the warm seasons of the year.

Hampshire piglets, with their characteristic white belt, feed from a farrowing pen. Hampshires were once called Thin-Rinds because of their thin skin and the low amount of fat on their backs. These piglets will grow into hogs with excellent reflexes and superior foraging skills.

Hampshire

This is one of the oldest breeds in America. They came to the United States from Hampshire, England, more than 150 years ago. Hampshires are easy to recognize. They are black pigs with a belt of white encircling their shoulders and each foreleg. They have a smooth profile and erect ears. Valued for their lean meat, Hampshires used to be the only hogs that were used to make Smithfield ham.

Landrace

These pigs are a relatively new breed in the United States. They came from Denmark in the 1930s but did not establish a foothold until the 1950s. Landrace are long pigs with a very smooth body. They have pink skin and white bristles. Their ears flop down so far that they nearly cover their eyes. Females produce a large litter and provide it with plenty of milk.

Poland China and Spotted Poland China
Despite its exotic name, the Poland China is all-American. It was developed in Butler and Warren counties in Ohio. One of its early breeders was of Polish background and some of the more notable early litters came from a sow allegedly named Old China. Poland Chinas are black, often with white markings. Those with more spots are called Spotted Poland China. They are a cross between a Poland China and Gloucester Old Spots, a pig brought form England in 1914. Spotted Poland Chinas can have more white than black. These are lean, hardy pigs with floppy ears.

Some thirsty Duroc piglets line up at a water-filled mud hole. Livestock raisers call Durocs the growth breed because they mature faster than any other. They are rugged, with sturdy bones, and most of them are hardy enough for almost any climate.

The Vietnamese pot-bellied pig is a breed of dwarf swine brought from Vietnam to the United States, Canada, and Sweden in the 1960s. Weighing in the range of 75 to 150 pounds (35 to 70 kilograms), this pig has become extremely popular, since it was introduced to the pet market in 1986.

A pot-bellied pig, its abdomen nearly touching the ground, forages in the grass. These pigs can live for up to twenty years.

A Tamworth sow yawns in the midday sun. It inherits its pigment from red Axford pigs imported from the West Indies. As a result, it rarely suffers from sunburn. Tamworths are comfortable in most climates, from the tropical areas of Southeast Asia to the cold pastures of Great Britain.

Tamworth

The Tamworth is one of the oldest purebreds. It is named after a town in central England that dates back to the early Middle Ages, when farming was a way of life for most people. All Tamworth are various shades of red. They have erect ears and long snouts and a relatively lean, long body.

Yorkshire

This pink-skinned, white-bristled pig has a very long body. It originated in Yorkshire County, England, about two hundred years ago. The Yorkshire was originally called a large white. Some of its more recent descendants, however, also have black spots on their skin. Yorkshires have very small, erect ears and short snouts. They raise large litters. Yorkshire are the most popular breed of pig in the United States.

Hereford

Herefords have white markings on a red body, like Hereford cattle. They are a cross between several other breeds, such as the Duroc, the Chester White, and the Poland China.

The need for body warmth or companionship sometimes encourages Yorkshires to double up on their sleeping hay. Such bonding can reverse itself at other times, occasionally resulting in squabbles. For this reason, hogs need space—to avoid each other when they're feeling competitive rather than intimate.

Dating back more than 150 years, the Tamworth is not only a very old breed, but it has changed less than any other. Hog raisers think of this red-coated animal as a typical bacon-type pig.

Purebreds are often seen at country fairs, where the competition is keen. This boy is posing with two prize Yorkshires, purebreds with smooth, healthy coats, and pleasantly rounded bodies— all of which may impress the judges.

Though not as attractive as their nature, pigs are nonetheless endearing to humans, who pose them, both artfully and artificially, for photographs that appear on posters, calendars, greeting cards, and an array of other products.

Selective breeding has created more than 370 domestic pig breeds, including the complex crossbreeds shown here. Hog raisers are aware that careful crossbreeding has many advantages over pure breeding. The process produces hogs that tend to reach market weight quickly.

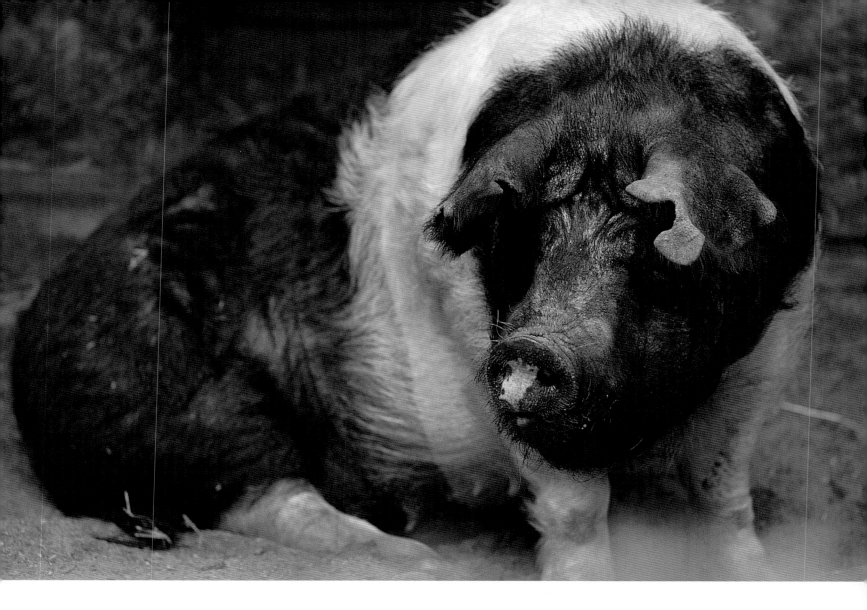

Crossbreeds

About 90 percent of the pigs in this country are the result of crossbreeding—either between two purebreds or between a crossbred sow and a purebred boar. Breeders go to the trouble of crossbreeding these animals over several generations in their search for hybrid vigor. Hybrid vigor describes those qualities that make an animal stronger, longer-lived, and more disease-resistant. Crossbreeding also leads to larger litters and higher weights at the time of weaning.

Mating

On a farm, pig breeding is usually managed rather than just allowed to happen. Even so, some piglets are stillborn and about a quarter of piglets are lost even before they are weaned. To minimize risks, breeders choose healthy boars with a good reputation for fatherhood and females with well-developed udders who come from a breed known for their mothering skills.

Boars are ready to breed by the time they are seven months old. From then on, many show great sexual vigor, being able to mate with dozens of sows within one breeding season. Gilts, which are females breeding for the first time, have their first estrus cycle when they are about nine months old, although most breeders wait until the female is a year old, to maximize the number of eggs produced. During their three-day period of estrus, females are in heat and can conceive. The vulva becomes swollen and reddish, and the animals tend to become restless. This three-day estrus cycle returns every eighteen to twenty-four days. Increasing the protein ratio of females' feed increases their ovulation rate.

The coquetry of the mating ritual usually involves avoidance of the male at first. The female flees the boar, who doggedly follows her, making grunting noises and sometimes salivating. There may be a small tussle before they settle down, during which the male nips lightly at the female's neck and ears.

Once the female has definitively accepted a boar's advances, she stops dead in her tracks, hunkering down and cocking her ears. A sort of tango often follows in which the two brush

An angler saddle hog from northern Germany. This black-and-white domestic breed is a mix of the Landrace and a hog known as the Wessex saddleback. These pigs are characterized by a white saddle of hair encircling the front of their bodies, and are found mostly in Schleswig-Holstein.

33

against each other and touch noses. Then they unite, remaining motionless for several minutes. Its not unusual for them to spend time close to each other afterwards, their heads side by side.

Breeders follow one of three methods when trying to mate pigs. In the handmating method, they simply place a sow and boar together during each day of the three-day estrus period and wait for them to mate. Penmating involves penning one boar up with ten females. Artificial insemination is a third technique. It is expensive and tricky and generally used only by professional breeders.

Once a female has become pregnant, gestation lasts approximately 114 days. Often dur-

In Illinois, a pig family engages in pleasant summer wading. Piglets need no convincing to imitate their parents when it comes to this activity. As these young pigs mature, the hair on their legs will increase. They will begin to look more and more like their elders.

ing the start of this period, the only way to tell that a gilt or sow is pregnant is if her repeated periods of estrus stop occurring. As it comes time to farrow, or give birth, her udders will become swollen with milk. A day or so before the event occurs, she will try to build a nest of straw or grass by shredding it with her teeth and plowing it into a pile.

Piglets

The babies are born with closed eyes. At birth the breeder removes their umbilical cords and cuts their "needle" teeth—the tiny teeth that might grow into boarlike tusks or hurt the mother's teats during feeding. What follows is a scramble for the teats, and once a baby piglet locks onto one, it will become his

A sow usually has enough nipples for all of her offspring—but not always. If there are too many piglets, the runt of the litter may find itself without a feeding station. It will then be up to the breeder to find a foster mother to take care of the outcast.

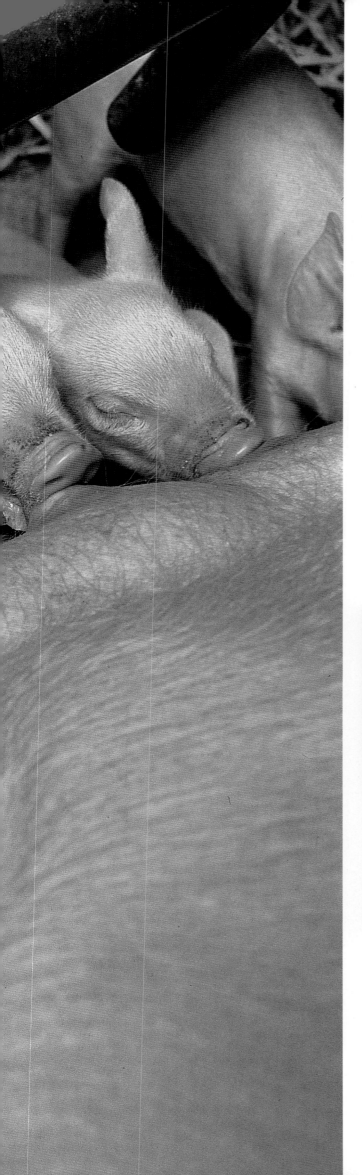

ordained place for the rest of the feeding. The boldest and largest will end up with the teat with the most milk, near the mother's head, and the runt usually ends up with a hind teat.

Piglets are completely dependent upon their mother's milk for about three weeks, although they can nurse for as long as three months. But as early as a few days after they are born, a mother may take them outside to introduce them to the pleasures of rolling around on damp earth or in mud. After three weeks they begin copying their mother as she digs for roots, worms, insects, and other types of food. Weaning, when it finally comes, can be a difficult time for the piglets, especially if it occurs early. For another two months they will come running to their mother like little children seeking protection. Their mothers will stand between them and any danger, whether it be a goose or an automobile.

Like most animals, female pigs and their offspring form very close bonds, as demonstrated by this mother, grazing the top of her piglet's head with a gentle kiss.

A sow may nurse as many as fourteen offspring at a time. Nursing does more than nourish the young. These newborn also receive antibodies in their mother's milk, that protect them against bacterial infections.

These Yorkshire piglets stay close together as they snooze. Especially during the first two weeks of their lives, and even some time thereafter, piglets need to be kept warm at a temperature ranging from 70 to 80 degrees Fahrenheit. Huddling together in a tight group accomplishes this.

When piglets are less than a few days old, their mother introduces them to the outdoors. Slowly but surely, they become less dependent upon her for food. However, a sudden feeling of in-security can send them rushing back to her teats for an impromptu nursing.

Struggling to free itself from the strong grip of a deep mud hole, this youngster is having one of its first experiences with water. Though not seen here, the mother is close at hand to offer assistance.

Following page:
Though small and vulnerable at birth, piglets grow up quickly. Within only six months, these two sleeping siblings will weigh as much as 220 pounds (100 kilograms) each.

A piglet sniffs a flower to determine whether or not it will make a tasty snack. Fortunately for horticulturalists, pigs are uninterested in blossoms, finding plant matter beneath the ground more to their liking.

Sows can be fierce in protecting their offspring. A mother observes conditions carefully before taking her piglets out to pasture. Any sign of danger can force her into a highly aggressive state.

The first venture into the outside world can be an overwhelming experience for piglets. At the beginning, they stay close to their mother. However, they will soon master the same behavioral skills she possesses and become more independent.

BOARS AND OTHER WILD PIGS

Wild pigs in the Americas are mostly descendants of domestic pigs that became feral and mated with the European boar. Because of this, the wild pigs of America come in many gradations of body shapes and a variety of colors. Some have the longer, thinner, hairier bodies of the true boar with its more elongated snout, while others are spotted and plump, looking more like farm pigs. It should be kept in mind, however, that both domestic pigs—feral or not—and the wild boar are descendants of the European boar, a wild forest creature that was never domesticated in as large numbers as the domestic pig.

Feral hogs—a mixture of boars and wild pigs—have been living in the forests of the United States since their arrival in the late fifteenth century. In the nineteenth century, wild boars were brought from Germany and Russia and placed on hunting preserves. From that point on, the two populations began mixing and producing hardy hybrids that have since made their way through most of the country. Already common in the forests of the southern United States, they've spread north along the east coast as far as New Hampshire and west toward Texas. In California, their population doubles every six years, due to the pig's rapid reproduction rate.

In the forests wild hogs and boars as well as their youngsters compete with bears, squirrels, and other animals for nuts, acorns,

The African savanna is a perfect environment for animals, such as the bush-pig, that tend to prefer dense cover. During the day the pig dozes in thickets, and when the weather is cooler, it finds warmth in comfortable beds of leaves.

A feral hog on a hillock in the Bahamas surveys the land below. The Caribbean pig population is thought to have begun with the few animals brought over by Columbus. This pig has maintained its close resemblance to the European boar, with its long snout, thick coat of bristles, and hair-covered ears.

plants, reptiles, and rodents. Because they are constant rooters, they dig up anything in sight, including certain species of native plants that may be endangered. Their rooting also causes erosion, a problem made even worse by the fact that these animals have no natural predators to limit their number. In Texas, the population of feral hogs has risen to an estimated one million.

In Europe, however, where the population of boar was once seriously endangered, conservationists see the rooting practices of their native boars as an advantage. This churning helps aerate the soil, adding nuts and seeds that may grow into plants. Europeans still remember a time when the wild boar almost became extinct, because hunters had eliminated vast numbers from the wild. The aggression of the boar as well as its speed made boar hunting a dangerous sport, but its thrills attracted noblemen throughout Europe, eager to prove their mettle. So popular was the sport, that by 1617, the last boar in the royal park at Windsor had been killed. After that, the British pastime of pig-sticking, as it was called, moved to India, where a large supply of animals and a plethora of servants made it a sport for gentlemen once again. Subsequent events have restocked some of the forests of other countries in Europe, but conservationists are aware that hunting of these animals cannot go unchecked.

A Chinese wild boar makes its way across an ice field. Male boars are known for the long distances they travel at night in search of food. When the animals hunt in a group, their movements sometimes develop into a migration, with the boars returning to a region they haven't visited for years.

Boars

Boars originally lived in Asia, but migrated to Europe and other countries by wandering or by being brought to these places by humans. Boars differ in appearance from domestic pigs by having straighter tails and small, pointed ears covered with hairs. The boar's head is more pointed than the pig's, with a long, flexible snout. The tail tends to be hairy, tufted at the tip by bristles. The body is narrower than the pig's, and males have a layer of skin over their shoulders called a shield that protects them from injury by thorns and attacking animals. Their silhouette slopes down to a smaller rear end, giving their body a torpedo shape.

A Southeast Asian wild boar stops to drink at a mud hole. The boar species is native to areas of thick forests and rugged terrain in Europe, Asia Minor, and North Africa. Over the years, it has been introduced by humans into New Guinea, New Zealand, and parts of North America.

A wild boar leaps through grasses across a stream. These large animals are surprisingly agile. Whereas a domestic pig might wade through the water or take another path, its feral cousin jumps over it. Wild boars are also excellent swimmers.

Distinguishing Features

The most striking difference between a boar and a domestic pig is the boar's four long canine tusks. The two upper canines, known as honers, curve out and up. The two lower canines, called rippers, curve up as well to touch the uppers, against which they are constantly sharpened. These tusks, which can tear roots from the soil better than a pitchfork, can also disembowel a medium-sized animal in one slash.

The hide of boars has long bristles over a woollier underfur. This fur runs from a dark gray to a rust brown. A boar's hair can become gray with age, but a few boars have silver-gray heads from the outset . Some boars are black or tawny colored. Young boars have six light stripes and five black stripes until they reach the age of six months. These stripes act as camouflage, protecting them from predators.

A boar's bristle coat gets thicker in winter to protect it from the cold. Along its spine is a narrow mane of longer bristles. The bristles and the boar's tough skin protect it as it crashes through forests and bushes, avoiding abrasions the way no other mammal's hide could.

On the average, boars tend to weigh from 100 to 200 pounds (45 to 90 kilograms), but boars weighing as much as 400 pounds (180

Wild boar piglets explore a conifer woodland. Light and black stripes serve to camouflage the young. They will lose their stripes at the age of six months, and become sexually mature twelve months after that. However, they will not be fully grown until they are five or six years old.

A European wild boar stops to drink at a pond. These animals are seldom spotted in daylight. Their keen hearing and sense of smell alert them to the presence of intruders. If challenged, they may attack an aggressor.

kilograms) have been found in the west; and in India, some boars grow to a weight of about 800 pounds (360 kilograms). Males tend to be somewhat larger than females.

Habits and Behavior

Wild boars love dense forest areas and mountain terrain, but they can adapt to the outskirts of wooded areas and even farmland. They cool off during hot weather by digging holes in the damp soil in which to rest; for, like all swine, they have no sweat glands. To escape cold, they build huge beds of branches and grass that look like giant birds' nests. Here, they may settle in with a partner to share body warmth.

In warm weather, boars use their sharp sense of smell and hearing to conduct their nighttime activities. As they search for food and avoid danger, boars prove themselves to be good athletes. They jump well and are good swimmers. They find their way through the forest by rubbing against trees, investigating the scent to find out whether other animals, including other boars, have passed through. If so, the ground around the trees will be littered with bristles.

In general, sows and their offspring congregate in herds of about twenty, known as drifts or sounders. Males spend their time alone, but also go foraging for food at night in packs of at least three, sometimes traveling several miles. The males return to the drifts during the rutting season in December and January, when many fights occur as the males compete for sexual ascendancy, sometimes suffering deep puncture wounds or broken tusks. In preparation for this time, the layer of protective skin on the males has grown thicker.

After mating is over, the males leave. The females stay in the herd for about three months out of their average 225-day gestation period. Then they find a secluded spot in which to give birth. A sow can have as many as twelve piglets. They are born covered with hair and with their eyes open. By a year and a half, they are sexually mature. At that time, the male offspring will leave the drift, returning only during the rut.

When boars sense a predator or other enemy, they have an ingenious way of organizing group protection. A herd may fan out, eventually curving completely around the opponent. Suddenly, the enemy finds itself surrounded by a ferocious defensive circle, trapped in the middle. At this point, it is the boars that may become the aggressors.

Because they will eat almost any kind of plant or animal, wild boars can survive harsh winters, rooting through the snow for leaves, roots, or frozen animals. In cold weather they build beds from branches and dried grasses to keep warm.

A wild boar nurses its offspring. Female boars have superb mothering instincts. They never leave their litter alone in the nest. When the piglets finally leave the nest, their mother always accompanies them. All adult female members of the mother's herd help in care and feeding.

This bearded pig is searching for fallen fruit, roots, or insect larva in a tropical forest in Borneo. This species prefers the lush envronment of the rain forest, but can survive in a wide variety of habitats,from beaches to cloud forests.

Other Wild Pigs

Boars and pigs share the genus *Sus,,* with seven other species. These range from the exotic-looking bearded pig, with its abundant chin whiskers, to the diminutive pygmy hog, scarcely 10 inches (25 centimeters) in height and no more than about 17 pounds (8 kilograms). Found in India, this miniature pig has only three pairs of teats, rather than the usual four teats of most pigs. Sadly, it now heads the list of some of the world's most endangered species, due to poaching and the disappearance of its habitat. Only two small, isolated populations of pygmy hogs remain in Assam. Attempts to reintroduce this species into the wild have mostly been failures. However, some initial attempts to breed these pigs in captivity have met with some success.

In Borneo, peninsular Malaysia, and Sumatra, the several subspecies of the bearded pig make their home. These sparsely haired pigs have the slimmest torso and the longest face of any of their kind. Their faces have two pairs of warts, but the front pair is concealed by their "beard" of thin, yellowish whiskers. Their two-tufted tail, which resembles that of an elephant, is unusual for swine.

In India lives another species of the *Sus* genus. It is called the Celebes pig, or Sulawesi warty pig. Celebes pigs are usually black with mixed yellow and white hairs, although a few are reddish brown or yellow. They have a tuft of hair on the forehead, and their snout is ringed by a yellow band.

Following page: A pair of red river hogs, natives of Central Africa, display the characteristic long tassels of white hair attached to the ears, as well as the black and white markings on the head, that create a white ring around the eye. The upper tusks of these animals are stunted, sometimes nearly invisible.

A rare sighting of an endangered pygmy hog in the state of Assam in northeast India. A small number of these miniature pigs, brought here from the wild, have been fed and mated in controlled conditions meant to simulate their natural habitat. Meanwhile, field studies of the animal's former habitat are in progress.

A Bornean bearded pig pauses for a moment in a field of grass. Note the thick, bristly chin whiskers and extremely elongated skull. These animals are still abundant in Kalimantan, East Malaysia, and Brunei, but their numbers are diminishing.

African Pigs

Two other genera of pigs similar to *Sus* are *Hylochoerus*, containing the forest hog species, and *Potomochoerus*, containing the bushpig and the red river hog. Forest hogs were first discovered in 1904 in a Kenyan forest. They range all over Central Africa. They have extremely coarse black hair covering their slate-gray bodies, with patches of it on their faces. Males have large warts under their eyes and large snouts. Their upper tusks, which flare outward, can reach a length of 1 foot (30 centimeters). Although they can weigh as much as 600 pounds (270 kilograms), they are not the best rooters. In order to survive, they need year-round supplies of fodder.

Bushpigs and red river hogs are very similar to the wild boar in the profile of their bodies, the shape of their snout, their bristles, and the stripes that camouflage the bodies of their young. However, bushpigs tend to show more variety in the color of their bodies, which are often black with white manes and gray faces.

Spread throughout parts of Africa and Madagascar in sounders composed of up to fifteen females, offspring, and one male, these animals prefer reed beds and thickets. They are incessant rooters who often do damage to crops. Red river hogs, also native to Central Africa, are distinguished by the strange tassels of hair dangling from their ears. It's possible that they may shake these as a way of threatening predators. They depend largely on elephants for their water sources. Once the elephants have dug for water in a forest clearing, taken their fill, and gone away, the red river hogs run to the water hole to take their turn.

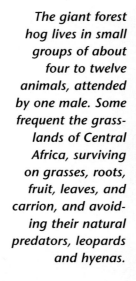

The giant forest hog lives in small groups of about four to twelve animals, attended by one male. Some frequent the grasslands of Central Africa, surviving on grasses, roots, fruit, leaves, and carrion, and avoiding their natural predators, leopards and hyenas.

A giant forest hog with its piglet. Females of this species go through approximately 150 days of gestation before producing two to six offspring. In about nine weeks, the young are weaned. The females mature quickly—in about a year—whereas males require more than three years to reach sexual maturity.

Found in southern Sudan, southern Ethiopia, Botswana, South Africa, Angola, Madagascar, and the Cormoros, the bushpig is a familiar creature of the grasslands. Its un- usually shaggy coat of mostly straight hairs can be any combination of gray, brown, or blackish brown.

This bushpig is about to fall prey to a leopard. Despite the pig's sharp senses and prodigious running skills, it is no match for the leopard's split-second timing. In a moment the leopard will sink its teeth into the pig's neck, and force it's victim to the ground with powerful paws.

African farmers dislike the bushpig, whose constant rooting often destroys crops. Unfortunately for the farmers, these animals do much of their food searching in the dead of night, when their digging is less likely to be disturbed.

A giant forest hog, wandering through a savanna in Kenya, is identifiable as a male by the two hairless, ball-shaped warts beneath its eyes. The disk of its snout is quite large, more than six inches (15 centimeters) in diameter.

WARTHOGS AND BABIRUSA

Even the most fervent pig enthusiast may find the appearance of two genera rather peculiar. Each of these animals startles the first-time viewer because of a peculiar body feature, and speculations as to why these adaptations have occurred have kept zoologists and evolutionary theorists busy. The first genus is the warthog (*Phacochoerus*), the male of which has two wartlike skin growths on either side of its head. The other is the babirusa (*Babirussa*), which has four tusks growing in a strange upward formation from its snout.

Warthogs

In the open country south of the Sahara, the traveler may see a sparsely coated slate– or clay-colored creature with a large shovel-shaped head and a broad muzzle. This is the warthog. Most striking are its tusks, which jut from the upper and the lower jaw. Most people will be able to distinguish the male from the female without any trouble, since male warthogs have two bizarre-looking skin protuberances on either side of the head. These enormous skin tags have no bone or cartilage, and at first glance, appear to have no function.

It takes more familiarity with the behavior of the warthog to deduce a purpose for its gigantic warts. During mating season, the adult males take part in extensive, highly ritualized battles, using their upper tusks, rather than their more dangerous lower tusks as weapons, as if, underneath the display of aggression, they really feared hurting each other. During these battles, an apparent function of the warts becomes evident. They work to cushion blows, while the males crash against each other repeatedly.

The warthog is sometimes known in Africa by the Swahili term ngiri. These animals are found in most open grasslands of Africa, south of the Sahara. Although the warthog's upper tusks seem more important than the lower ones, it is the sharp lower tusks that are used to inflict injury on enemies.

For further protection, warthogs have skin of a nearly impenetrable thickness. Although they have few bristles, they have cheek whiskers, a tufted tail, and a mane of long dark hair. The fact that the glands in their eyes tend to exude a flow of liquid doesn't help their appearance. The fluids leave dark stains on their faces. Females lack both the runny eyes and the large warts of males. They are smaller, too, and have shorter tusks.

Feeding and Defense

In northern and southern savannas and in nearly arid zones, warthogs cover about 4 miles (6.5 kilometers) each day while the sun is up, grinding green grasses with their molar teeth and hinge jaw and using their snout to dig up roots, tubers, and bulbs, as they rest on callused knees. Sometimes they eat carrion or bark from the trees, and when the grasses are dry they dig for the rhizomes—rootlike growths—buried under the surface. In fact, so unequaled is their talent for finding these buried nutritional treasures and removing them from the soil, that as many as seventy-eight warthogs can find enough food to survive in a 2-square-mile (5-square-kilometer) habitat. They also eat fallen fruit. Essential to their survival is a nearby water source where

This African warthog and the three red-billed oxpeckers riding on it have a perfect symbiotic relationship. Ticks on the warthog's body are a food source for the birds. In return, the birds keep the irritating ticks from becoming too numerous.

they can drink and wallow. If they live near farmland, the farmers consider them a threat, for they can do damage to crops.

Warthogs move at a moderate speed, though they can run at over 30 miles (48 kilometers) per hour when they sense danger—which may be a pursuing cheetah, wild dog, or spotted hyena. As the warthogs run, their tails sticks straight up. Occasionally, they may stop in their tracks and turn on their predator, challenging it with their tusks. By that time, their offspring have probably found a hole to hide in. As long as they stay in the hole, they are safe from danger; but when they emerge the next morning, they may find a lion waiting for them.

At night the females and their offspring go to sleep in burrows often left behind by aardvarks, while the males spend an extra hour or so after dark, looking for more food, especially if the moon is out. No one knows for certain if warthogs are totally dependent upon aardvarks for their burrows, since warthogs are good diggers and could conceivably build their own sleeping quarters.

Caring For Young

Warthogs are sociable animals. They live in family groups in territory that is not open to other families. Each population is divided into clans, which consist of sounders of approximately four to six warthogs, although sounders of many more have been seen. Mothers and daughters up to the age of two years may stay together in the same sounder. Each sounder is likely to have more than one mother, and these show kinship by suckling each other's offspring. They lie close to one another in their burrows and even lie against each other outside during cold weather. Sometimes, warthogs rub tusk glands together or use their snout and incisors to groom the mane of a partner, who lies stretched out with its legs raised—the traditional grooming position.

The young spend part of their time playing, sparring aggressively, and running after each other in games that will establish rank order by the time they are grown. Submissive warthogs identify themselves by lowering

In apparent bliss, this warthog is rolling over and over in a pool of mud. The action applies a coat of mud to the warthog's body, which insulates it against the sun and protects it from insect bites.

While warthogs find safety from predators in their underground burrows, they must be wary when they come out for food. Lions will often wait patiently around the entrance to a burrow, and then pounce ferociously at the first sign of the emerging warthog.

Two warthogs lock heads over possession of a mud wallow. Though competition among warthogs exists, most fighting is ritualized or playful, employing display and sparring rather than actual violence. The lower tusks are rarely, if ever, used to slash or stab another warthog.

their head and mane, flattening their ears, and backing away while making a squealing sound. Mother and offspring greet each other by rubbing noses and grunting. When it's time to go back to the burrow, a mother calls her piglets, using low, gentle-sounding grunts. If piglets ever feel they are in danger, they will signal their mother with squeaking noises.

Males separate from females as the males mature, but they always remain within home range. Young males up to four years generally stay with other male warthogs. The males are known for their springy, hip-rolling walk. They keep their tails out and bent down. Sometimes they nuzzle and massage each other, scentmarking each other's head, sides,

or rear. A male warthog rests at times with its chin on the rump of another male.

When a sow is in heat, the males join her sounder. The males stay up late into the night, sniffing for burrows in which females are sleeping. Then they wait for them to awaken in the morning, presenting themselves to the females as they climb from their burrows. During the mating ritual, males fight each other, rarely causing serious damage. In savannas, mating occurs as the rains end. Pregnancy lasts for as long as 170 days, after which the rainy season begins again. In wet, equatorial regions, there is no specific breeding season.

When it is time to farrow, the sows stay in their burrows, producing two to eight hairless piglets. Six or seven weeks later, the piglets begin following their mother out of the burrow, trailing behind her in an orderly line. They will return to their mother for milk regularly, until they are weaned at six months.

Since the nineteenth century, the fast-moving warthog has been hunted by safari for its tusks, for its meat, and for sport. Hunting has all but eliminated them from South Africa, although their numbers in other parts of Africa are not yet seriously threatened. Nevertheless, some countries have recently passed conservation laws to protect them.

Babirusa

If a warthog draws one's attention because of its skin protuberances, a babirusa makes itself just as noticeable because of the strange formation of its tusks. The upper canines of the male penetrate the skin of its nose and curve over the front of the face toward the forehead. No other mammal has such a tusk formation. The mandibular canines cover the front of the face as well. Because these tusks stick up, they remind some people of the antlers of a deer. Such a confusion of tusk with antlers has led to the babirusa's name, which means "pig deer." Singular as the babirusa's tusks are, there are no certainties about their function. The lower tusks seem to be designed for slashing, but both pairs of tusks are brittle. They shatter easily and seem rarely to be used for very aggressive fighting. The purpose of the upper tusks is also a matter for debate. Natives of Sulawesi, in Indonesia, claim that the babirusa

use them to hook lowhanging branches to support their heads while at rest. Certain naturalists maintain that the upper tusks are merely a kind of fender, which protects the eyes and throat of the animal during mating periods, when the males engage in fights.

Aside from its strange-looking tusks, a babirusa looks a lot like the common farm pig. Its legs are a little longer, and its ears are quite small, although babirusa have keen hearing. What is more, only a little knowledge about the habits of the babirusa in the wild exists, for these pigs are exceedingly shy and often elude observers. They live in swamps and thick jungles along rivers and lakes in groups of five to fifteen. Their brownish-gray, nearly hairless skin and torpedo-shaped bodies blend in well with their habitat. Unlike the noisy boar, they move quietly through the forest, withdrawing into the underbrush at the first sign of danger. They are good swimmers and have been known to swim to other islands in search of fruit, leaves, water plants, and insect larvae. Like most other kinds of swine, they enjoy wallowing in mud.

Living in Isolation

The babirusa are isolated cousins of the rest of the swine family. Their distribution is limited to Sulawesi, which has been cut off from the mainland of Asia for millions of years. Perhaps because of their isolation, babirusa have several other qualities not found in typical swine. Their litters, born in about five months, are surprisingly small—only about one to three offspring instead of the usual four to eight. This characteristic may have developed for the same reason the babirusa's unique tusks did. Babirusa originally had few predators. Therefore, it was not necessary to produce many offspring. Also, unlike many other wild piglets, the offspring of babirusa do not begin life with striped bodies. As if they had little need for protection, they wander away from their mother in search of solid food at the early age of ten days. Babirusa also

Following page: A warthog indulges in a cooling ritual. Having dug down to damp earth, it is finding relief during the hottest period of the day. Being half-buried won't, however, protect it from potential enemies. For this, it depends upon complete concealment in an underground burrow.

Like most pig species, babirusa enjoy rolling in mud or bathing. They feel at home in any body of water, and are adept swimmers. Some repeatedly swim to offshore islands in search of mates.

have a more complex stomach than most swine. It has two chambers, which probably allows them to digest fiber the way that cattle and sheep do.

In the wild, babirusa have become critically endangered by hunters and by the destruction of their habitats. Hunting of babirusa has been occurring since prehistoric times with the use of nets, spears, and dogs. Recently, large-scale logging has represented the greatest threat to these animals. Logging exposes them to dual disadvantages. They lose their habitat and are also more exposed to hunters and their dogs. In areas of large logging operations, babirusa are one of the first animals to become locally extinct.

Pigs Today

In common with many other creatures, pigs in the wild are under threat, due to human incursion and exploitation. Though the domesticated pig is far from being an endangered animal, its living conditions are part of an increasing concern over the care and raising of all food source animals on a mass scale. Uncrowded , unstressed animals are happier and healthier, and provide higher-quality milk, eggs, and meat.

As if to prove their versatility at last, pigs are moving into new areas and sometimes becoming stars in their own right. New York's Greenwich Village boasts its own neighborhood pig, that can be seen in the early morning walking with its mistress through the area's narrow streets and small parks. In other places, pigs have been taught to retrieve, run races, and pull carts. Swimming pigs and their annual water ballet are the pride of San Marcos, a small town in Texas, that claims to be the home of the Swine Dive.

Then, of course, there is the popular recent film, featuring a determined and rebellious talking pig, that has changed a number of long-held misconceptions. It may be that this fictional but charming animal may bring more people to an increased understanding of not only pigs, but of the nature of all living things and their place in the world.

Although some paleontologic data link the babirusa more closely to hippos than to true pigs, the species is still classified as a member of the pig family.

The wild boar has a characteristically bullet-shaped body, which is much narrower than that of a domestic pig. The animal shown here has auburn bristles shielding its mostly dark brown under-fur. Its snout is extremely elongated, and capable of energetic rooting.

INDEX

*Page numbers in **bold-face** type indicate photo captions.*

Plus

Dinosaurs and Prehistoric Animals

Allosaurus

by Helen Frost

Consulting Editor: Gail Saunders-Smith, PhD

Consultant: Jack Horner
Curator of Paleontology
Museum of the Rockies
Bozeman, Montana

Capstone
press

Mankato, Minnesota

Pebble Plus is published by Capstone Press,
151 Good Counsel Drive, P.O. Box 669, Mankato, Minnesota 56002.
www.capstonepress.com

1 2 3 4 5 6 10 09 08 07 06 05

Library of Congress Cataloging-in-Publication Data
Frost, Helen, 1949–
    Allosaurus / by Helen Frost.
    p. cm.—(Pebble plus—dinosaurs and prehistoric animals)
    Includes bibliographical references and index.
    ISBN 0-7368-3646-2 (hardcover)
    1. Allosaurus—Juvenile literature. I. Title. II. Series.
QE862.S3F77 2005
567.912—dc22   2004011090

Summary: Simple text and illustrations present allosaurus, its body parts, and behavior.

Editorial Credits
Martha E. H. Rustad, editor; Linda Clavel, designer; Jon Hughes, illustrator; Wanda Winch, photo researcher;
    Scott Thoms, photo editor

Photo Credit
Bruce Coleman Inc./Danilo Donadoni, 20–21

The author thanks the children's library staff at the Allen County Public Library in Fort Wayne, Indiana,
for research assistance.

Note to Parents and Teachers

The Dinosaurs and Prehistoric Animals set supports national science standards related to
the evolution of life. This book describes and illustrates allosaurus. The images support
early readers in understanding the text. The repetition of words and phrases helps early
readers learn new words. This book also introduces early readers to subject-specific
vocabulary words, which are defined in the Glossary section. Early readers may need
assistance to read some words and to use the Table of Contents, Glossary, Read More,
Internet Sites, and Index sections of the book.

Table of Contents

A Strong Dinosaur

Allosaurus was a strong
dinosaur. It had a big head
with a bump over each eye.

Allosaurus lived

in prehistoric times.

It lived about

150 million years ago

in North America.

How Allosaurus Looked

Allosaurus was about as long as a fire truck. It was about 38 feet (12 meters) long.

Allosaurus had a long tail.
It held its tail off
the ground when it ran
or walked.

Allosaurus had long legs
and short arms.

What Allosaurus Did

Allosaurus hunted and ate other animals. It used sharp claws to kill other animals.

Allosaurus bit its food.

Its teeth were sharp
and curved.

Allosaurus had a large, strong mouth. It opened wide to swallow food.

19

The End of Allosaurus

Allosaurus died out about
135 million years ago.
No one knows why they
all died. You can see
allosaurus fossils in museums.

Glossary

claw—a hard curved nail on the foot of an animal or a bird

dinosaur—a large reptile that lived on land in prehistoric times

fossil—the remains or traces of an animal or a plant, preserved as rock

hunt—to chase and kill animals for food

museum—a place where interesting objects of art, history, or science are shown

North America—the continent in the Western Hemisphere that includes the United States, Canada, Mexico, and Central America

prehistoric—very, very old; prehistoric means belonging to a time before history was written down.

Read More

Cohen, Daniel. *Allosaurus.* The Bridgestone Science Library: Discovering Dinosaurs. Mankato, Minn.: Bridgestone Books, 2003.

Dahl, Michael. *Strange Lizard: The Adventure of Allosaurus.* Dinosaur World. Minneapolis: Picture Window Books, 2004.

Goecke, Michael P. *Allosaurus.* A Buddy Book: Dinosaurs. Edina, Minn.: Abdo, 2002.

Internet Sites

FactHound offers a safe, fun way to find Internet sites related to this book. All of the sites on FactHound have been researched by our staff.

Here's how:

1. Visit *www.facthound.com*

2. Type in this special code **0736836462** for age-appropriate sites. Or enter a search word related to this book for a more general search.

3. Click on the **Fetch It** button.

FactHound will fetch the best sites for you!

Index

Word Count: 130
Grade Level: 1
Early-Intervention Level: 14